Animals in the Wild

Zebra

by Mary Hoffman

Raintree Childrens Books
Milwaukee • Toronto • Melbourne • London
Belitha Press Limited • London

Zebras are part of the same family as horses. Young zebras are called foals, the same name used for baby horses. But they look different from horses. They have black and white stripes.

Zebra foals can stand about an hour after they are born. They stay close to their mothers until they are strong enough to run. Mothers are called mares. They carry their foals for about a year.

Year-old foals still drink milk from their mothers. Some mares have foals every year. Foals know their own mothers.

Zebras live in groups, called herds. A herd
has one male zebra—the stallion. It also
has up to six mares and their foals.

The hair along a zebra's neck stands straight up instead of hanging down like a horse's mane. Stripes go up to the mane.

Every zebra has its own pattern of stripes. Zebras know each other's patterns. The stripes are not exactly the same.

Burchell's zebras are the most common. There are about 300,000 of them living in the wild of Africa. Another zebra is the Grévy's zebra. Grévy's zebras live in Africa, too, but there are more Burchell's zebras.

Grévy's zebras are taller and heavier than Burchell's zebras. Grévy's zebras have big, round, furry ears and long legs. Their stripes are narrower. They are hard to see in tall grass.

Lions eat zebras when they can catch
them. Zebra herds move from place to
place to find grass to eat. They may
wander over more than 100 square miles.

Little birds often travel with them. Fork-tailed drongoes sit on the backs of zebras and eat insects that the zebras kick into the air.

Burchell's zebras have shadow-stripes.
Zebras need long drinks once a day.

They drink water at water holes. Some zebras have to travel far for water.

Dry dust can be useful. Zebras roll in dust
to scratch their backs.

Zebras nibble each other's backs to get rid
of insects that cause itches.

Young male zebras live together until they start their own herds. When a young female comes around, stallions bite and kick each other. When one has had enough, he lowers his head and trots away.

Most of the time zebras get along well.
They also get along with other animals.
They share water holes with kudu and
giraffes. But people cannot tame or train
zebras.

First published in this edition in the United States of America 1985
by Raintree Publishers Inc., 330 East Kilbourn Avenue,
Milwaukee, Wisconsin 53202.

First published in the United Kingdom under the title
Animals in the Wild—Zebra
by Belitha Press Ltd.,
2 Beresford Terrace, London N5 2DH
in association with Methuen Children's Books Ltd.

Text and illustrations in this form © Belitha Press 1985
Text © Mary Hoffman 1985.

Library of Congress Number: 84-24793

Dedicated to Jessica.

Scientific Adviser: Dr. Gwynne Vevers. Picture Researcher: Stella Martin

Acknowledgements are due to Bruce Coleman Ltd for all photographs in this
book with the following exceptions: NHPA p. 5; Survival Anglia pp. 6/7, 12/13,
14, 15 and 20; Oxford Scientific Films pp. 10, 17; Natural Science Photos p. 8

ISBN 0-8172-2414-9 (U.S.A.)

Library of Congress Cataloging in Publication Data

Hoffman, Mary
   Zebra.

(Animals in the wild)
   Summary: Describes the life and habitat of the zebra, with emphasis on
its struggle for survival.
   1. Zebras—Juvenile literature. (1. Zebras)
I. Title II. Series.
QL737.U62S47 1985   599.72'5   84-24793
ISBN 0-8172-2414-9

1 2 3 4 5 6 7 8 9   89 88 87 86 85